I NEED TO DO WHAT?!

I NEED TO DO WHAT?!

A Wedding Guide for the Groom, Best Man, & Ushers

by: G. C. Van Deusen

Published by Tryke Books

I Need to Do What?!
A Wedding Guide for the Groom, Best Man, and Ushers

Copyright 1987 by G.C. Van Deusen

Printed in the United States of America
All rights reserved. No part of this book may be used or reproduced in any manner whatsoever without written permission except in the case of brief quotations in critical articles and reviews.
For information address Tryke Books, P.O. Box 42392, Cincinnati, Ohio, 45242
Designer: Karen Gibbs

Library of Congress Cataloging in Publication Data

Van Deusen, Glenn C.
I Need to Do What ?!
A Wedding Guide for the Groom, Best Man, and Ushers
Includes index.
1. Weddings   2. Wedding Planning   I. Title
392'.5   87-50733

ISBN 0-9619066-7-7 Softcover

ACKNOWLEDGMENT

Special thanks to Beth, Bill, Carla, Don, Kurt, and Marjorie for their assistance and advice.

NOTICE -- DISCLAIMER

This book provides information on the subject matter covered. It is sold with the full understanding that neither the publisher nor author are engaged in legal or professional services. If such expert assistance is required, seek a professional.

The purpose of this book is not to provide all the information available regarding the subject but to expand and supplement other sources.

Every effort to maintain accuracy has been made; however, this does not ensure perfection. Therefore, this book is best used as a general guide. The author and publisher shall have neither liability nor responsibility to any person or entity with respect to any damage or loss caused or alleged to be caused directly or indirectly by the information in this book.

CONTENTS

Chapter	Page
Introduction	8
Part I: The Groom
1 An Overview of the Wedding	13
Part II: The Best Man
2 The Best Man's Duties	19
3 Before the Wedding	21
4 The Wedding Day	31
5 The Reception	35
Part III: The Ushers
6 The Ushers Duties	45
7 Before the Wedding	47
8 The Wedding Day	53
9 The Reception	67
Appendix A Quick Reference
(Names and Phone Numbers)	68
Appendix B Best Man's Checklist	70
Appendix C Car Decorating Suggestions	72

INTRODUCTION

Congratulations!

A very special day is rapidly approaching. Whether you are planning your own wedding or have been asked to be a Best Man or Usher at a friends wedding, this book provides a complete run-down of what is typically expected of the men in the wedding party, so that you can help make the day run smoothly.

Being selected as a Best Man or Usher is a distinct honor but also a big responsibility. You've been asked to help orchestrate the most important day in a person's life, their wedding day.

While this book addresses the standard or traditional practices associated with a wedding, it should be remembered that each wedding is unique and should be tailored to best serve the wishes of the principal characters -- the Bride and Groom.

Therefore, this book should be considered a reference guide and not an absolute set of rules. Whether this will be your first opportunity to be an attendant at a wedding or you're a seasoned veteran, you should discover numerous tips which will at most leave with you with a feeling of pride in doing a job well and, at the least, prevent you from making a mistake that could embarrass you and others.

While this book thoroughly reviews what would be expected of you at a formal wedding, many items discussed apply to even a simple in-home wedding.

Above all else, remember that while you may have been asked to help serve as an attendant, you have also been asked to participate in a joyous celebration of two people entering a new life together, so enjoy yourself -- weddings are serious, but they should also be fun!

The first half of this book is tailored to the functions of the Best Man, and the second half is devoted to the Ushers. Of course if you are the Groom, your familiarity with the functions of your attendants is a must to keep things running smoothly. You will find that this book's step-by-step format easily guides you through all the activities that lie ahead.

PART I

THE GROOM

CHAPTER I
AN OVERVIEW FOR THE GROOM

Many changes are about to take place in your life as a result of your upcoming marriage. This book will help you ease into the first big event, your wedding day. No two weddings are alike, nor should they be, each is an expression of the individuals involved. The suggestions and advice offered in this book should not be considered "must do" items, but rather helpful hints to make your wedding day go smoothly. This book primarily reviews what you and your groomsmen will need to know and do for the actual wedding ceremony. Of course, a significant amount of your time will soon be (or already has been) occupied with such things as: selecting the location for the ceremony, compiling a guest list, writing newspaper announcements, selecting food and entertainment for the reception, purchasing gifts for your groomsmen, and developing a budget, to name just a few.

By time your actual wedding day arrives, there should be very little you will need to do, if your Best Man handles things properly. He will coordinate most of the activities for the men in the wedding. Of course, your bride-to-be, and her family, will generally take care of everything else.

However, you do need to work closely with the Best Man ahead of time to plan the day's events and ensure that everything is in order. Quite often, you may find it easier, or even necessary, to take care of some of the Best Man's duties yourself. Therefore, your familiarity with his duties is a must. In reviewing these duties together, you will probably choose to ignore some of the more formal, or old-fashioned wedding practices.

Obviously, with so much to do, you will want to choose a Best Man that you can rely on to get things done. The person you select to be your Best Man should therefore have strong organizational and planning skills. While such qualities are preferred, and may relieve you of many headaches, it could be more important for you to have a very special friend or relative as Best Man, regardless of their managerial skills. The trade-off involved clearly can only be decided by you.

An Overview for the Groom

As an option, I have seen weddings where two Best Men are involved and found that such an arrangement can work very well, particularly if one of the men lives out of town, making day-to-day chores more difficult to accomplish. The unique skills and interests of each of the men combined also can often work to your advantage.

Again, it is more important that your wedding day be enjoyable and not simply "according to the rules." After all, rules were made to be broken. Enjoy.

PART II

THE BEST MAN

CHAPTER II
THE BEST MAN'S DUTIES

The Best Man is an indispensable part of any wedding and one of the busiest people at the ceremony. While he is generally a brother or very close friend, his ability to effectively manage and coordinate numerous activities is the primary reason for his selection.

No longer is the Best Man selected simply because of his size or brute strength, as was typical in medieval days when the Best Man's primary function was to ward off unwanted guests and keep the Bride and Groom together in safety.

Of all the male attendants at a wedding, the Best Man has the most extensive responsibilities. He assumes responsibilities as varied as: travel agent, witness, valet, toastmaster, messenger, secretary, advisor, coordinator of the Ushers, and chauffeur.

On the day of the wedding, the only thing that should be of concern to the Groom is arriving for the ceremony on time. The Best Man should take care of all of the Groom's other needs.

While the Best Man often assists in planning the wedding, and perhaps even the honeymoon, his range of duties will vary largely based on the amount of time he has to spend with the Groom before the ceremony and his proximity to the actual wedding location. However, on the actual wedding day, the Best Man should try to free the Groom of as many chores as possible so that he can fully enjoy his wedding day without worrying about details.

The following chapters will take you a step at a time through the planning and actual participation in the wedding. Since many of your responsibilities involve coordination with the Ushers, you also should thoroughly read Part III "The Ushers."

CHAPTER III

BEFORE THE WEDDING

Although the numerous details of the wedding day may seem endless, proper planning ahead of time will make the day run smoothly. Under ideal conditions, the Best Man would be notified at least two months before the big day.

As soon as possible, the Best Man should review with the Groom such items as wedding attire, lodging for out-of-town ushers, boutonnieres, the marriage license, and the bachelor party. Each of these items will be discussed in detail.

WEDDING ATTIRE

If the decision is made to wear clothes which most of the attendants will have to rent, the Best Man may assume the responsibility to determine the best shop to provide the clothing. In many cases, the Bride and Groom will take care of this themselves. (How formal the men's clothes will be is dependent on the Bride's attire.) If tuxedos are being rented, to make the best appearance, all the men should obtain their clothes from the same store. This will mean that the Best Man will need to coordinate fittings and make sure that each Usher's measurements are submitted in time to avoid having to make last minute alterations.

A quick reference sheet is provided in Appendix A to help keep track of the many people you will be working with during the next several weeks.

LODGING

Four to six weeks before the wedding the Best Man should make lodging arrangements for any out-of-town ushers. Extra time may be necessary if the wedding will be held at a popular resort or during a peak occupancy period. If many of the attendants are on limited budgets, and know the Bride or Groom's family, they may simply stay at their homes.

FLOWERS

The Best Man should make arrangements to have boutonnieres for the Groom, himself, and the ushers available the morning of the wedding (the actual flowers used are typically selected by the Bride). The Best Man may also arrange for flowers for the fathers of the Bride and Groom. The Groom's boutonniere is usually a flower that is also used in the Bride's bouquet but different from that of the Best Man and Ushers.

Although they are being used less and less these days, gloves may be included in a very formal wedding. The Groom and the Best Man would wear their gloves until they get to the altar, but typically remove them during the ceremony to simplify the handling of rings. The Ushers would wear their gloves throughout the ceremony.

THE MARRIAGE LICENSE

The Best Man along with the Maid of Honor are typically the official witnesses for the Bride and Groom when obtaining their marriage license. It is also the responsibility of the Best Man to be keeper of the marriage license for delivery on the wedding day to the person officiating the marriage ceremony.

Marriage licenses are typically valid for only a limited time (often 60 days from date of issue). Therefore, the Best Man should ensure that the license is not obtained too far in advance of the ceremony. It is best to check with your local licensing bureau for details.

The Best Man should also ensure that the Bride and Groom have made an appointment for a blood test, if the state that the wedding will take place in requires one, before applying for the marriage license. Sometimes it takes several days before the results are available.

GIFTS

As members of the wedding party, the Best Man and Ushers typically offer a gift to the Bride either individually or by pooling their resources. They also typically provide a gift to the Groom or may offer one major gift to the couple. The gifts are traditionally given either at the Bachelor Party or the Rehearsal Dinner and are generally either household items or personalized gifts bearing the names or signatures of the attendants.

THE BACHELOR PARTY

A Bachelor Party can be handled in numerous ways, either offered by the Best Man to the Groom and attendants, by the Best Man and attendants for the Groom, and in some cases even by the Groom to his attendants. Further information regarding the Bachelor Party is discussed later. If the Best Man is involved in coordinating this party, it is again advisable to plan well in advance if a restaurant, club, or hotel is to be used for the party.

EXPENSES

The Best Man is expected to pay for his own travel expenses (if he is coming from out of town for the wedding), his wedding clothes, a gift for the Bride and Groom, and occasionally a portion of the Bachelor Party. However, there are generally many exceptions to these guidelines. For example, if clothes are not rented for the wedding, the Groom traditionally provides the Best Man with his gloves, tie, and boutonniere.

Although it shouldn't be expected, the Groom may pay for the Best Man's lodging if he is from out of town. As previously mentioned, the Best Man may also join with the Ushers to offer a gift for the Bride and Groom from all the male members of the wedding party. This second gift is entirely optional, and in many cases not offered.

Although rather uncommon, if money is of no concern to the Groom he may offer to pay for all his attendants clothes and a portion of or all of the Bachelor Party expenses.

THE FINAL WEEK

During the week before the wedding, the Best Man's time is largely spent confirming prior arrangements and taking care of a host of miscellaneous details. The one new item this week will be to coordinate the Ushers at the rehearsal.

As part of his supervision of the Ushers, the Best Man should: confirm that boutonnieres have been ordered and will be available, provide the Ushers with directions to the ceremony and reception (including a map for each Usher if necessary), give each Usher a list of guests who should receive special attention in seating, and ensure that clothes for the men in the wedding have been ordered, fitted, and altered.

The Best Man's responsibilities to the Groom during the final week include helping the Groom pack for his honeymoon, ensuring that the car to be used by the newlyweds to leave the reception (if applicable) is in proper order -- particularly if the couple is driving on their honeymoon, taking into his possession any airline or cruise tickets (also not forgetting the marriage license), confirming reservations for the honeymoon, helping pack a separate bag of clothes for the Groom to use when making his getaway from the reception to the honeymoon, and participating in the wedding rehearsal.

The Best Man's involvement in the rehearsal is very similar to the Ushers and is detailed in Chapter Seven. Other miscellaneous responsibilities include collecting from the Groom the fee for the wedding official and any assistants or musicians.

While a fee is not necessary for a clergyman, it is a common practice to offer a donation which can range anywhere from $20 to several hundred dollars depending on the size of the wedding, the financial situation of the couple, and local practices. The simplest way to check on what would be appropriate is to call the secretary at the official's office to find out what is normally expected.

The payment of fees or tips (the Groom's expense) should be new bills placed in a plain envelope, delivered by the Best Man just before the start of the ceremony. The Best Man should also check with the Bride this week to determine the time that she will be arriving at the church the day of the wedding to ensure that the Bride and Groom do not see each other before the wedding starts.

As a final note, more and more couples are planning dramatic exits from their weddings (such as leaving by horse-drawn carriage, balloon, boat, etc.). Obviously, if this will be true at the wedding you attend, further advance planning will be necessary. Also, you should not feel left out or overlooked if some of your tasks are taken over by the Bride or Groom, it may simply be easier for them to handle.

THE GUEST BOOK

Although a wedding guest book is not a must, many couples find it a welcome addition at the reception and a nice sentimental reminder after the wedding day. Acquiring the book and arranging for someone to attend to it during the reception may also be the duty of the Best Man.

Any book could be used, however, most stationary or card shops sell books specifically for this purpose which allow each guest to sign their name and offer a brief comment if they so desire. If properly placed in the reception area, the guest book can also help break up the monotony of the guests waiting in the receiving line to congratulate the happy couple.

The book should be placed on a small table with a white table cloth and two chairs for guests to use while signing. The table could be attended by a young family member who perhaps because of their age was not able to participate as an attendant in the wedding. However, it is not necessary to have an attendant.

While the Maid of Honor may prefer to coordinate this task, it is best to check before the wedding to see if you will be expected to be responsible for the guest book. If there is a guest book attendant, they should be instructed to feel perfectly at ease to ask people to sign the book and not wait for them to notice that it is available.

ADDITIONAL POINTERS

Although not necessary, it is often a touching gesture for the Best Man to have a small gift waiting for the newlyweds on their wedding night. This may be a bottle of wine, champagne, flowers, etc.

Before the Wedding

Unless limousines have been ordered to transport the wedding party to the ceremony and then to the reception, the Best Man should help coordinate cars and drivers to ensure that no one is left stranded. If friends and relatives are used for transportation and there is a considerable distance to travel, the Best Man should consider offering to pay for gas or providing a small gift for the extra assistance.

Since Bridesmaids and Ushers are typically paired for the recession following the wedding, they may also ride together to the reception. Whatever decision is made for the transportation of the wedding party, make sure that everyone is clear as to who should be with whom and has specific directions and maps if necessary.

As a final but very important reminder, if limousines are going to be used, be sure to provide transportation home for those people that rode to the wedding in the limousines since they will likely not be available after the reception.

A complete checklist of items which you are likely to be responsible for as a Best Man is provided in Appendix B.

CHAPTER IV
THE WEDDING DAY

Hopefully, by this time all your prior planning and organization have paid off and you are ready to devote your full attention to the Groom. It is your responsibility to see that he is properly dressed and delivered to the ceremony at the proper time. Your day may begin by waking the Groom and staying at his side during the entire day to resolve any last minute problems, lend moral support, or just provide companionship.

GROOMING THE GROOM

In addition to laying out his clothes, the Best Man should ensure that the Groom is perfectly dressed and groomed before leaving for the ceremony. This may include having extra buttons, a needle and thread, collar stays, shoe laces, or comb available in case of an emergency. As a final step, the Best Man should ensure that the Groom's boutonniere is placed over the button hole on his coat lapel.

PACKING LUGGAGE

The Best Man should help the Groom pack any remaining items necessary for the honeymoon as well as packing a separate bag to change at the reception before leaving for the honeymoon. The Best Man should ensure that the Groom's getaway bag includes any necessary travel items such as tickets, passports, claim checks (if the honeymoon luggage has already been delivered to the hotel), and that the bag will be in a safe place at the reception (out of the reach of practical jokers).

THE RING

The Best Man should carry the Bride's ring in his vest pocket or on his little finger to be presented to the Groom at the appropriate time during the ceremony. If the Best Man is to receive the ring from a Ring Bearer, it is advisable to lightly sew the ring to the Ring Bearer's pillow to avoid any accidents (particularly if the Ring Bearer is a young child).

AT THE CHURCH

The Best Man and Groom should arrive at least 30 minutes before the ceremony is to begin and wait in the vestibule or whatever separate room may be set aside for the Groom. The Best Man should then briefly leave the Groom to make sure that the Head Usher has properly briefed all the Ushers and made sure that they are properly dressed. (The Ushers should have arrived for the service at least one hour ahead of time to receive their boutonnieres, light candles if necessary, and seat early guests).

The Best Man should also take this time to deliver the sealed envelopes with gratuities or fees to the wedding official, musicians, etc. The envelopes should be presented in the name of the Groom. The Best Man should then get back to the Groom as quickly as possible to see if he requires any further assistance.

If the Groom arrives for the ceremony wearing a hat or top coat, the Best Man should take them to a place where they will be ready for the Groom following the recession and before stepping outside.

OFF TO THE RECEPTION

After the ceremony, the Best Man should get the Bride and Groom off to the reception as quickly as possible. The reason for getting to the reception quickly is so that any pictures to be taken of the wedding party can be done and the receiving line set-up without unnecessarily delaying the guests. Quite frequently, there will also be pictures taken where the ceremony was held. If this is true for you, simply try to keep things moving along. Of course, all of this should be done without appearing rushed or hectic. It's advisable to have the photography session before the reception rather than after so that everyone is captured when they are still looking their best.

Unless the reception is in a nearby room, the cars to transport the wedding party to the reception should be available as soon as the newlyweds exit the building. The Best Man should already have arranged for transportation to the reception for the Bride and Groom (who will ride by themselves in one car), himself, and the remainder of the wedding party. If a driver for the Bride and Groom is not available, the Best Man should chauffeur.

CHAPTER V
THE RECEPTION

While the remaining responsibilities of the Best Man are beginning to dwindle, he still has several important duties to perform at the reception. These duties are primarily: 1) offering the first toast to the Bride and Groom and 2) ensuring that the newlyweds get off to a smooth start on their honeymoon.

Both of these items are discussed below, but first a few minor points regarding the beginning of the reception.

THE RECEIVING LINE

After completing the photography session, the receiving line is typically the first activity at a reception. The purpose of the receiving line is to make sure that every guest has the opportunity to meet with the newlyweds and their families and offer congratulatory remarks in person. The Best Man is not included in the receiving line but instead mingles among the guests and helps the families of the newlyweds in any way possible. The Best Man may also take this time to make a last minute check on the Bride and Groom's luggage, tickets, and get-away clothes. The Best Man also may work with the Ushers to decorate the Bride and Groom's car. Suggestions for decorating the car are listed in Appendix C.

The Best Man should periodically check back with the Groom to see if he needs any help and possibly remind him of specific comments he wanted to make to individual guests.

SEATING ARRANGEMENTS

If the reception includes a seating, the Bride and Groom along with the Best Man, Maid of Honor, Ushers, and Bridesmaids are typically seated at one table. The Bride and Groom sit in the center with the Bride on the Groom's right. The Best Man sits on the Bride's right while the Maid of Honor sits on the Groom's left. The Ushers and Bridesmaids alternate on either side of the Best Man and Maid of Honor.

THE TOAST

The Best Man traditionally has the privilege of making the first toast to the Bride and Groom. The toast may be made at any time after the receiving line has been completed and everyone has been given a glass to drink to the newlyweds. The toast is generally made with champagne or wine but even ginger ale can be used so that everyone can participate. Everyone except the Bride and Groom should stand for the Best Man's toast. Regardless of how good a public speaker he may be, a Best Man should limit his toast to a very brief remark. Typical toasts include "To Wayne and Nelleke, may they enjoy a long, happy, healthy, and prosperous life together;" "May their happiness shared today continue through the years;" or "May the love and joy that brought these two here today intensify as they share their new life together." However, the most appropriate toast is always one that comes from the heart and possibly mentions something unique about that couple.

The Best Man may also take this opportunity to tell a few short stories or reflect on his past friendship with the Bride and Groom. However, any topic which could even slightly embarrass anyone at the reception or detract from this special day should be avoided.

The next toast is offered by the Groom to his Bride while also offering thanks to the Best Man. After the Groom's toast, the Best Man may ask if anyone else would like to offer a toast. However, because some people are very embarrassed when asked to speak in public, the Best Man should never point out someone and ask for a toast unless an arrangement has been made to do this prior to the reception.

Another good time for the Best Man to offer the first toast is after the cake cutting ceremony, when everyone's attention has been directed to the newlyweds.

After all the toasts have been completed, the Best Man may read any telegrams or messages that have been received. Whether or not messages are read aloud should be decided by the Bride and Groom before the wedding day.

DANCING

Although there may not be dancing at all receptions, it is generally included to add to the festive celebration. As the music begins, the "first dance" is conducted by the Bride and Groom. At this time, they have the dance floor to themselves and generally make a complete circle of the room. To keep with tradition, a set order of dancing and partners is followed. These dances usually only last for a few minutes, and not for an entire song, with several couples dancing at the same time and continually cutting-in.

The traditional dance order is: the Bride and Groom (first and by themselves); followed by the Bride and her father, the Groom and the mother of the Bride; the Groom's father and the Bride, the Groom and his mother. Next, the parents dance with each other while the Bride dances with the Best Man and the Groom with the Maid of Honor. Once this is completed everyone in the wedding party should join in the dancing.

As Best Man, you should also dance with the Bride's mother, the Groom's mother, each of the Bridesmaids, and as many of the guests as possible. To encourage all of the guests to dance, it may be a good idea to arrange for specific pairings of Ushers and Bridesmaids ahead of time for at least the first two dances. People will usually start to dance when they see a number of other people dancing.

If there will be a long receiving line at the reception, there is no reason why music and dancing cannot be going on while the families receive guests so that those who have already been greeted can enjoy themselves. If this is the case, when it comes time for the "first dance" the Best Man should request that the dance floor be cleared for the Bride and Groom.

PREPARING FOR DEPARTURE

After the traditional tossing of the bridal bouquet and garter, the Best Man should help the Groom change into his going-away clothes and ensure smooth departure to the honeymoon. You should help the Groom change and collect his wedding clothes for either safe keeping or return (if they were rented). At this time you should provide the Groom with car keys, wallet, tickets, passports, hotel keys, etc.

Your next responsibility is to alert the parents of the Bride and Groom that their children are about ready to leave on their honeymoon and escort the parents to the dressing rooms so that they can spend a few moments with their children before they leave. During this time you should arrange for transportation to be brought to the front of the reception hall, double check that all luggage has been properly cared for, help pass out confetti, bird seed, rose petals, or rice to be showered upon the newlyweds as they depart, and prepare a clear path for the Bride and Groom to exit through the guests.

It is also perfectly acceptable to provide this "shower" for the Bride and Groom as they leave the marriage ceremony on their way to the reception. This may even be preferred if the reception will only be attended by a small group of people.

TIME TO RELAX

With the Bride and Groom now safely on the way to their honeymoon, the Best Man can finally start to relax. At this point, the only remaining responsibility is to gather any clothes which were rented for the ceremony, along with those of the Groom, and return them to the rental shop.

PART III

THE USHERS

CHAPTER VI
THE USHER'S DUTIES

This section addresses the duties and responsibilities of being an attendant in a wedding in the role of an Usher. Although not nearly as complicated as the responsibilities of a Best Man, there are still numerous tasks expected of an Usher. Strict adherence to these guidelines is certainly not necessary, however, awareness of what the Bride and Groom may expect of you can only help you feel more confident and relaxed in your role as a member of their wedding party. Your selection as an Usher is a privilege to participate more fully in a very important celebration of a friend or relative.

The number of Ushers at a wedding is dependent upon the number of guests expected and the number of Bridesmaids. There will usually be one Usher for every 40-50 guests. Although there may well be more Ushers than Bridesmaids, you can count on the Bride to arrange for each Bridesmaid to have a male escort.

If there are several Ushers in attendance, the Groom will typically appoint a Head Usher to oversee the rest of the group.

The Usher's Duties

You may hear the term Junior Usher. This refers only to the person's age. Ushers are typically about the same age as the Groom, as is the Best Man. Junior Ushers, therefore, are usually in their middle teens and quite likely relatives of the Bride or Groom. Their duties are no different than those of the adult Ushers.

The Head Usher is usually selected because of his ability to recognize most of the guests attending the ceremony and be aware of their special seating needs (discussed in a later section). Therefore, even if you are a best friend or roommate, you should not feel bad if you are not selected for this task. It is more practical and advisable for the Groom to select a Head Usher based on that person's familiarity with the guests.

CHAPTER VII
BEFORE THE WEDDING

The preparation before a wedding for the Ushers is very simple. There are really only two items which require much attention several weeks before the wedding. The first is determining what the attire will be so that measurements can be taken if clothes will need to be rented. The second is to arrange for the bachelor party (if one is to be given by the Ushers) as well as purchasing any gifts for the Bride and Groom. Both of these items are discussed in the following sections.

THE WEDDING ATTIRE

The Ushers wear the same style of clothes as the Groom and Best Man. If clothes are to be rented, the Best Man should arrange for one shop to provide all the clothes for the men in the wedding (to present the most polished appearance) and he should advise you of the lead time necessary for alterations. As an Usher you should comply with the Best Man's request to submit sizes and attend fittings as far in advance as possible. Ushers are typically responsible for the expense of renting clothes although if the wedding attire calls for suits, then ties, gloves, and boutonnieres are typically provided by the Groom. Further discussion of the expenses you are likely to incur can be found in the section "Expenses."

If the wedding is local, then arranging for rental clothes is simply a matter of stopping by the store that was selected to provide the clothing. If you will be attending an out of town wedding, the procedure is also quite simple. You can visit any good men's clothing store or a tailor in your area and explain that you need to be measured for a wedding -- they will generally be very accommodating. The measurements should include: neck, chest, sleeve, waist, inseam, outseam, and shoe size. Remember also to check your hat and glove size in case such apparel will be used.

With this information in hand, a quick call to the Best Man should take care of everything. To be on the safe side, you should try to visit the actual rental shop sometime before the wedding (even the night before if that's the only time available) to try on the clothes.

THE BACHELOR PARTY

The bachelor party originated as an opportunity for the Groom to have one last fling "with the boys" before his wedding. Although bachelor parties were often held the night before the wedding, it is now more typical for them to be held several days in advance so that if the party gets a little carried away, people will have time to recover before the wedding.

Since the bachelor party is designed as the one last fling before being married, it is unusual to have a bachelor party for someone that is not marrying for the first time.

The bachelor party may take any number of forms and be offered by the Groom, the Best Man, the Best Man and Ushers, or any combination of the above. While bachelor parties have acquired a reputation as being wild, drunken, free-for-alls, in actuality most bachelor parties are much more subdued and allow the Groom to share in the comradery of his friends and bolster his (in all likelihood) somewhat shaky nerves.

Before planning a bachelor party be sure to check with the Groom and see if your efforts will be appreciated. Sometimes, the Groom would opt not to have another party before the wedding or would prefer to combine the bachelor party with the bride's party for her bridesmaids.

If a bachelor party is planned, it can be held at the Groom's house, in a club, hotel, restaurant, or possibly in a back room of a nightclub where you don't have to worry about disrupting other guests.

There are traditionally two activities that take place at a bachelor party. The first is the Groom's toast to his Bride. The second is the Groom's presentation of gifts to his attendants (this could also take place at the rehearsal dinner). Typical of the rest of the party, these events do not follow any particular format or occur at any particular time.

Following the toast to the Bride, the Groom would traditionally either crack the stem of the glass, throw the glass over his shoulder, or throw it into a fireplace so that it could never be used for a less honorable purpose. While this custom is not widely followed today, if it is followed by the Groom then the attendants should follow his lead. Obviously, if the party is at a bar or club, it would be advisable to notify the owners ahead of time that this will take place.

Other than the traditional toast to the Bride, and the distribution of gifts, there is, as mentioned, no set procedure for a bachelor party. However, there is typically a good deal of creativity that is exhibited at these parties.

Activities could range from the simple offering of toasts to the Groom, poker games, dancing girls, a "roast," showing of old home movies from the Groom's parents, or a tour of all of the Groom's old stomping grounds. If any travel is to be involved on the night of the bachelor party, it is a very good idea to rent a van <u>and</u> a driver to ensure the safety of everyone involved.

EXPENSES

As previously mentioned, the Ushers are responsible for the expense of renting clothes, if necessary, to match the Groom's wedding attire. Ties, gloves, and boutonnieres will be provided by the Groom if suits are being worn. Although it is rather rare, the Groom may offer to pay for the Ushers' clothes if rental is involved.

The Ushers pay for their own travel expenses to the wedding but the Groom may provide for their lodging. Other expenses include a gift to the Bride and Groom, a share in a gift offered from the Ushers as a group (optional), and if necessary, a share in the expense of the bachelor party.

THE REHEARSAL

The duties of the Ushers at the rehearsal are quite simply to find out where they should stand, who they will be paired with in the procession and recession, and who will handle the aisle canvas, bows, and ribbons (to designate reserved seats). The rehearsal also may well be the first chance for all the wedding attendants to meet each other and is usually followed by a dinner given by the Groom's parents.

While all together, the rehearsal may also be a good time for the Ushers to determine what type of decorations they may want to use for the newlyweds' car. It is advisable to discuss this with the Bride and Groom rather than starting off their honeymoon on a sour note by doing something that they may disapprove of or may damage the car. Even simple things such as tape, soap, and shaving cream can damage a car's finish and therefore great care should be taken. Simple items, which are very effective, include wrapping paper streamers on the car, or writing on the <u>glass only</u> with white shoe polish. Additional car decorating suggestions are provided in Appendix C.

A popular trick years ago, which may no longer be as effective today, due to the wide-spread use of self-service gas stations, was to include a small note on the gas cap alerting the attendant that the occupants of the car were newlyweds. In some cases, the Bride and Groom would go for weeks without realizing how everyone somehow knew they were newlyweds.

CHAPTER VIII
THE WEDDING DAY
PREPARING FOR THE CEREMONY

The Ushers should all arrive at least an hour before the ceremony, affix their boutonnieres, and wait as a group at the left of the inside door of the church or hall. By standing on the left side, the Ushers are prepared to offer their right arm to arriving guests. If hats or topcoats are being worn, they should be removed before greeting the guests. If gloves are being used, they should be put on at this time.

At this time the Head Usher should ensure that all of the Ushers are aware of who the guests are that will require special seating arrangements and which guests are to be included in the first few reserved rows. This may be accomplished either by providing each Usher with a list of names or reminding them to ask the guests for their pew cards (reserve seat passes distributed prior to the ceremony).

The Head Usher should also reconfirm that the Ushers responsible for extending the aisle runner or draping the ribbons along the ends of the pews understand their duties.

To make sure that all the Ushers are properly dressed and arrive for the ceremony at the correct time, it is often a good idea to have everyone meet early in the day and dress at one place. However, it may not be a good idea to all drive to the ceremony together, as extra cars may be needed after the ceremony to transport bridesmaids and guests to the reception or back home again. As a final check, the Head Usher may wish to ask the Bride the morning of the wedding if any additional guests have been included in the special seating section.

GREETING THE GUESTS

The Ushers primary responsibility, as would seem obvious, is to seat the guests. The Ushers should do this in a friendly, relaxed, and expedient manner. The Ushers should never appear to be rushed even when, as typically happens, a large group of people all arrive to be seated at once.

As each guest enters, an Usher should step forward to greet them. Typically, the guest will identify themselves as either a friend of the Bride or a friend of the Groom, or present a pew card. If this procedure is not followed, you should politely ask if they are a "friend of the Bride," or a "friend of the Groom."

The Usher would then offer his **right** arm to a female guest or simply lead the way for a male guest to the best available seat. If a woman is accompanied by a husband and/or family, you should still offer your right arm to the woman and she would be followed by those accompanying her. Although not as traditional, it seems perfectly acceptable for a husband to walk beside his wife while she is being escorted by an Usher. However, the husband should never walk on the left side of the Usher.

If several female guests arrive at the same time, and there are not enough Ushers available to escort them individually, an Usher should offer his arm to the eldest female guest and ask the others to follow or he may (which may be a better solution so as not to identify the wrong woman as the eldest) ask the other women to wait until he or another Usher is available to escort them.

While the entrance of guests is typically a "feast or famine" situation, the Ushers should always try to maintain a relaxed, unhurried appearance and take time to quietly talk with the guests as they escort them to their seats. A brief friendly conversation with the guests (even if only about the weather) is far better than a cold, impersonal march down the aisle.

If space is limited or Ushers are numerous, it may be a good idea to have a traffic pattern established ahead of time where Ushers use only the center aisle for seating guests and then return to the back by another aisle to avoid confusion or a head-on collision.

If a man should arrive unaccompanied by a woman, the Usher would not extend his arm to the man but simply determine where he is to be seated and then lead the man to his seat (with the Usher always remaining to the left of the guest). An exception to this would be if the man should need assistance due to age or illness. If more than one man arrives at once, the eldest man should walk directly behind or to the side of the Usher, followed by the younger man.

It is important to remember that your responsibility is to be of assistance to the guests and not to be a drill sargeant. Therefore, if a guest should prefer not to follow this traditional seating procedure, you should be pleasant and accommodating.

The Wedding Day

SEATING THE GUESTS

Even if you do not recognize the guest you are seating, it is polite to exchange some pleasantries, whether it be about the wedding, the weather, or whatever.

If you have reason to believe that person should be seated in the first few rows, but they have not indicated so, it is much better to ask them if they have a pew card rather than to seat them in the wrong section.

Until the ceremony begins, no invited guests at a wedding should be allowed to seat themselves.

For the most part, guests are seated according to where the parents of the Bride and Groom sit. Namely, the Bride's family and guests sit on the left while the Groom's family and guests sit on the right. The exception to this regards reserved rows (which will be discussed later) and situations where there may be far more guests of one family than the other. In this case, it is the responsibility of the Head Usher to see that if one side begins to look very crowded while the other side is almost empty, then the guests, regardless of their relationship to the families, should be seated evenly on both sides.

The easiest way for the Ushers to handle such a situation is to say that "guests are being seated on both sides for the ceremony" and then lead the guest to the best seat in the sparsest section. The Ushers may also mention "If you wouldn't mind, there are much better seats available on the other side." This is a perfectly acceptable procedure and will be familiar to most of the guests. The largest contributor to this possible unevenness in guests is typically merely a function of the ceremony being held much farther away from where one of the families lives than the other.

RESERVED ROWS

As an Usher, you will need to be aware of who should be seated in the reserved rows. Fortunately, you were spared the decision of who to include, or the more difficult issue, who not to include. This will all be determined in advance by the Bride and her mother. The reserved rows are set aside for family members and very close friends of the family.

The first row on each side of the aisle is reserved for the Bride's parents (on the left side facing forward) and the Groom's parents (on the right side facing forward). Beyond the first row, there may be any number of reserved rows. However, just as the Ushers should make sure that the room is filled evenly on the left and right, there will also be the same number of reserved rows on each side of the aisle. In the case where the Groom, for example, may need only two reserved rows while the Bride requires six, the final set up should be four reserved rows on each side of the aisle.

The Wedding Day

The guests designated for the reserved section would then fill those rows on a first come, first served basis. The reserved rows are often identified by a small floral arrangement or ribbon placed next to the aisle.

Once most of the guests have arrived and been seated, hopefully 10 to 15 minutes before the start of the ceremony, the parents of the Groom are escorted to their seats by the Head Usher. Traditionally, the father sits on the aisle.

About five minutes before the start of the ceremony, the mother of the Bride is escorted to her seat. It's a good idea for someone to notify the Groom at this time that the mother of the Bride has been seated so he is aware that the ceremony is beginning.

The Head Usher again typically escorts the mother of the Bride to her seat, unless one of her sons (the eldest, if more than one) is an Usher, in which case he would escort his mother.

Seating the mother of the Bride signifies the start of the ceremony and no other guests should be escorted to their seats. If other guests do arrive they should quietly find their way to a seat in the back.

The Head Usher should then have the two previously designated Ushers care for the aisle runner and pew ribbons. The aisle runner is usually a white linen or plastic roll which is placed at the head of the aisle and rolled out for the wedding party to walk on. The purpose of the aisle runner is to prevent the train of the Bride's wedding gown from getting soiled. Care should be taken not to jerk on the runner and pull it loose from the front step. These same two Ushers should then walk to the last of the reserved rows to pick up the white ribbon that has been folded there and, proceeding towards the rear, drape the ribbon over the end of each row.

The reason to drape a white ribbon over the ends of the rows is to indicate that no one should seat themselves by way of the center aisle after the mother of the Bride has been seated and also prevent guests from exiting the ceremony before the Bride and Groom. However, such ribbons are being increasingly omitted from weddings.

If ribbons are used, at the end of the ceremony, after the recession has been completed and the guests in the reserved rows have exited, the Ushers should remove the ribbons starting from the front. This allows the guests who arrived earliest for the ceremony to be the first to depart.

SPECIAL SEATING ARRANGEMENTS

When the parents of either the Bride or Groom have been divorced, it may require a slight adjustment in seating arrangements. Otherwise, this could create a

The Wedding Day

rather tense situation, depending on how friendly the parents have remained. However, the parents should be able to put aside past grievances for the brief time that the ceremony will last, so their children can thoroughly enjoy their wedding day.

In either case, it is not the responsibility of an Usher to intervene or decide on seating, this should all have been decided well in advance. This section has only been included so you will understand the traditional protocol.

Regardless of how friendly divorced parents may have remained, they are not seated together. Rather, the mother is seated in the first row either by herself or along with close friends and relatives. The father sits in the next available row behind the mother. Again, if you know such a situation exists be sure to check with the Head Usher for specific directions ahead of time.

If the Bride or Groom's parents are deceased, a close relative or friend may take their place in the first row or it may be left empty. Again, these decisions should have all been made earlier by the Bride and Groom. Regardless of who is chosen to occupy the mother of the Bride's seat, they are the last person seated.

When seating guests in a partially occupied row, the guests who arrived early are not expected to move in and give up their better seats. However, all guests are typically seated from the center aisle.

THE PROCESSION

Once all the guests are seated, the Ushers next responsibility is to lead the wedding procession. The Ushers, as well as the Bridesmaids, are paired by height with the shortest Usher standing at the head of the procession followed by the taller Ushers. Next comes the Bridesmaids, Maid of Honor, Ring Bearer and Flower Girl, Bride and Father of the Bride.

The exception to the height rule is if Junior Ushers and Bridesmaids are involved, in which case Junior Ushers follow adult Ushers and Junior Bridesmaids precede adult Bridesmaids. If there is an uneven number of Ushers or Bridesmaids, the unpaired person follows rather than leads their group.

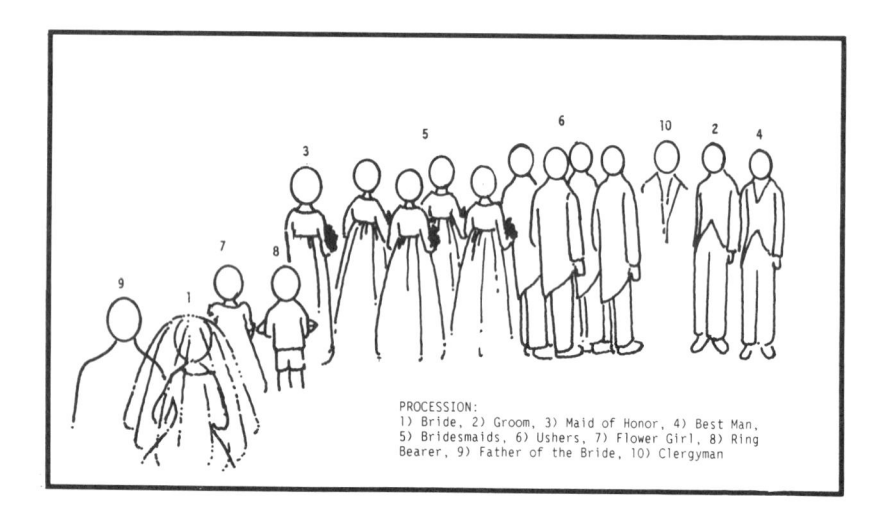

PROCESSION:
1) Bride, 2) Groom, 3) Maid of Honor, 4) Best Man, 5) Bridesmaids, 6) Ushers, 7) Flower Girl, 8) Ring Bearer, 9) Father of the Bride, 10) Clergyman

Although called the wedding march, the wedding party does not actually march, but rather walks at a slow, even pace. Even at the most formal weddings, the old hesitation step is no longer used as at best, it looked very awkward.

Each pair of people in the procession should follow about four rows behind the group in front of them. While this sounds rather regimented, that is not the impression you want to make on the guests. Instead, you should smile and be a reflection of the joy that the ceremony is all about. Although you may want to glance at your friends as you pass them, because you are there to serve the Groom, your glance would best be directed towards him as he awaits his Bride.

When you reach the place where you will stand, you should slowly turn to watch the Bride as she approaches. On the day of the wedding, all of this should come very naturally since it will probably have been practiced several times at the rehearsal. The actual place and position that the Ushers assume once the Bride has completed the procession will vary from one ceremony to the next and will generally be decided by the Bride.

RECESSION

The Bride and Groom will lead the recession, followed by the Ring Bearer and Flower Girl (if present), Best Man and Maid of Honor, and then the Ushers and Bridesmaids.

Unlike the procession, each Usher usually escorts a Bridesmaid down the aisle, with the shortest again followed by the tallest. This practice is used to symbolize the joining of man and woman in the marriage that just took place. Also, like the procession, an unescorted Usher would follow behind the last pair of adult Ushers.

Any Junior Ushers or Junior Bridesmaids would follow behind the adults. It is also acceptable for a lone Usher to walk between two of the adult couples.

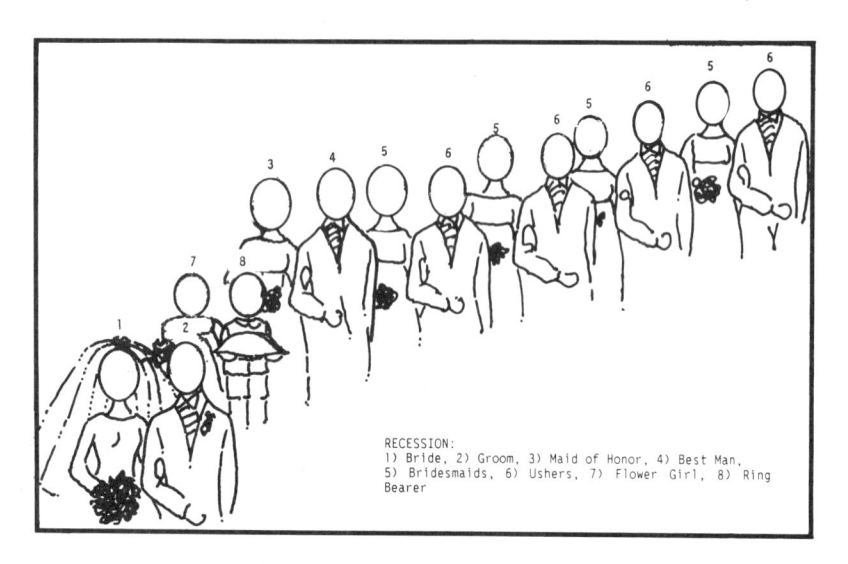

RECESSION:
1) Bride, 2) Groom, 3) Maid of Honor, 4) Best Man, 5) Bridesmaids, 6) Ushers, 7) Flower Girl, 8) Ring Bearer

The Wedding Day

Once the recession has been completed a previously assigned Usher should return to escort the Bride and Groom's mothers (the mother of the Bride first) and special guests from their seats and then take up the pew ribbons. Depending upon the wishes of the Bride, only the mothers may be escorted out, with the remainder of the guests in the reserved rows asked to follow them rather than waiting for the Ushers to return.

As the Ushers help the remaining guests to exit, the Best Man will assist the Bride and Groom in either having their pictures taken, establishing a receiving line, or getting off to the reception.

As soon as all the activities at the wedding site are completed, the Ushers should quickly proceed to the reception, remembering to take any Bridesmaids or special guests with them. In some cases, limousines will be provided for the Ushers and Bridesmaids and therefore eliminate this responsibility.

CHAPTER IX
THE RECEPTION

The completion of the wedding ceremony was essentially the completion of the Ushers duties. As an Usher, your primary concern at the reception is to have fun and usually dance with as many of the Bridesmaids as possible, and of course the Bride. You may also be asked to help with coats, refreshments, or other miscellaneous chores.

Ushers do not stand in the receiving line but do sit at the bridal table. The Ushers sit on either side of the Bride and Groom, alternating seats with the Bridesmaids. You may also want to prepare a small toast to the Bride and Groom.

At the end of the reception, you may assist in distributing the rice, rose petals, bird seed, confetti, or whatever is to be showered upon the Bride and Groom as they leave for their honeymoon.

As a final but important reminder--have fun and enjoy this very special day!

APPENDIX A
QUICK REFERENCE

Use these pages to keep track of the other members of the wedding party as well as businesses and services involved in the wedding. This list may include the florist, reception hall, photographer, travel agent, tuxedo shop, etc.

Name − Address	Telephone
Zip Code	
Zip Code	
Zip Code	
Zip Code	
Zip Code	
Zip Code	
Zip Code	
Zip Code	

Name – Address	Telephone
Zip Code	
Zip Code	
Zip Code	
Zip Code	
Zip Code	
Zip Code	
Zip Code	
Zip Code	
Zip Code	
Zip Code	
Zip Code	
Zip Code	
Zip Code	

APPENDIX B
BEST MAN'S CHECKLIST

Things to do Before Wedding

Six Weeks
- ____ Reserve lodging for yourself and Ushers
- ____ Select shop for wedding clothes rental
- ____ Coordinate fitting and/or measurements for clothes
- ____ Begin planning Bachelor Party
- ____ Assist in honeymoon plans

Four Weeks
- ____ Order boutonnieres for yourself, Groom, Ushers, Fathers
- ____ Witness marriage license (then keep in safe place)
- ____ Decide on gifts for Bride and Groom
- ____ Arrange blood tests (if necessary)

Two Weeks
- ____ Prepare car for honeymoon trip
- ____ Select wedding gifts
- ____ Buy a "guest book" and arrange for an attendant

One Week
- ____ Receive payment for wedding officials from Groom
- ____ Confirm when Bride will arrive at Church
- ____ Provide Ushers with maps to ceremony and reception
- ____ Prepare toast/speech
- ____ Complete final fitting of rental clothes
- ____ Assist at the wedding rehearsal
- ____ Determine if telegrams should be read at the reception
- ____ Purchase decorations for Bride and Groom's car

Day Before
___ Give ushers a list of guests requiring special seating
___ Pack Groom's "getaway" clothes
___ Prepare an "emergency kit" of: needle and thread, shoe laces, comb, etc.
___ Confirm time to wake/meet Groom
___ Help Groom pack for honeymoon, checking for tickets, keys, passports, etc.
___ Receive money from Groom for gratuities/fees

Wedding Day
___ Make sure boutonnieres are available
___ Deliver marriage license
___ Ensure that all members of the wedding party have transportation to the reception
___ Deliver gratuity/fee to the wedding official, musicians, etc.
___ Secure wedding ring in a safe place
___ Collect any telegrams or messages to be read at the reception

Day After
___ Return rental clothes
___ Relax!!

APPENDIX C
CAR DECORATING SUGGESTIONS

The key to good car decorating is to remember to carry-over the festive mood of the day and not do anything that would require substantial effort on the Groom's part to make the car safe to drive or in any way damage the car. Again, this assumes that the Bride and Groom have previously consented to this activity (the Best Man should check).

However well intentioned, some decorations can become major headaches. Perhaps the largest problem area involves the car's paint. Even simple tape left on a car in a particularly hot climate can be damaging.

Here are some tried-and-true options. But don't stop with these, use your imagination.

- Stuff interior with balloons
- Tie streamers on antenna, door handles, bumpers, etc.
- String cans to back of car
- Write on windows with white shoe polish (not windshield)
- Trim with flowers (real or paper)
- Place a humorous or "just married" sign on the rear bumper or trunk
- Attach a Bride and Groom figure (like on the cake) to the hood ornament.
- Run streamers through hubcaps
- Draw faces of Bride and Groom on side windows

INDEX

A

Advance planning, 13, 21
Aisle runner, 54, 59-60
Aisle traffic, 56

B

Bachelor party, 24, 49-51
Blood test, 23
Boutonniere, 22, 31
Bridal gift, 24
Bridal table, 36, 67

C

Car decorating, 36, 52, 72
Chauffeuring, 34
Checklist, 70-71
Clothes:
 Get-away, 26, 32, 39
 Wedding, 21, 47-48
Clothes
 measurements, 21, 48

D

Dancing, 38-39, 67
Donation to Clergyman, 26
Dramatic exits, 27

E

Emergency kit, 31
Expenses:
 Groom's, 24-27, 49, 51;
 Best Man's, 24-25;
 Ushers, 48, 51

F

Fees/Gratuities, 33
First dance, 38
Flowers for men, 22
Formal procedures, 13

G

Gifts, 24, 28, 51
Gloves, 23
Greeting guests, 54-56
Guest book, 27-28

H

Head Usher 45-46, 53, 57, 60
Honeymoon car, 26
Honeymoon gift, 28

J

Junior Bridesmaid, 62
Junior Usher, 46, 62

L

Last person seated, 59, 61
Late arrivals, 59
Limousines, 29
Lodging leadtime, 22

M

Maps, 25
Marriage license, 23

INDEX

N

Number of ushers, 45

P

Pew card, 55, 57
Pew ribbons, 59-60, 65
Photographs, 33-34
Procession, 62-63

Q

Quick reference
 list, 68-69

R

Receiving line, 35-36, 67
Recession, 64-65
Rehearsal, 25
Reserved rows, 58-59
Responsibilities:
 Groom, 13;
 Best Man, 19;
 Ushers, 45
Rings, 32
Rules: Wedding, 13

S

Seating arrangements, 36, 53, 57-58
Seating men, 56
Seating the parents, 58-59
Selecting a Best Man, 19
Special seating, 60-61

T

Telegrams, 38
Toasts, 36-37, 50
Transportation:
 To Wedding, 29;
 To Reception, 29, 33-34
Travel planning, 26, 39-40

U

Uneven guest
 seating, 57-58

W

Witnesses, 23

NOTES

NOTES

NOTES

For additional copies of I Need to Do What?!, check your local bookstore or use this convenient order form.

Tryke Books
P.O. Box 42392
Cincinnati, OH 45242

Please rush me _____ copy (copies) of I Need To Do What?!

NAME: _____

ADDRESS: _____

CITY: _____ STATE: ____ ZIP: _____

I have enclosed $5.95 for each copy.
Ohio residents add 5 1/2% sales tax.

Please add $1 for shipping and handling of the first book ordered and 50¢ for each additional copy.

Send check or money order payable to **Tryke** (no cash or C.O.D.'s).

Please allow 3-4 weeks for delivery.

	Example	Your Order
Book(s) Ordered	2	
Book cost ($5.95 each)	$11.90	$
5 1/2% Tax (if in Ohio)	$ --	$
Shipping and Handling ($1 for first book, 50¢ for each additional)	$ 1.50	$ ___
TOTAL	$13.40	$